PEACE

BOOKS BY GILLIAN CONOLEY

PEACE
THE PLOT GENIE
PROFANE HALO
LOVERS IN THE USED WORLD
BECKON
TALL STRANGER
SOME GANGSTER PAIN

Chapbooks:

AN OH   A SKY   A FABRIC   AN UNDERTOW
EXPERIMENTS IN PATIENCE
FATHERLESS AFTERNOON
WOMAN SPEAKING INSIDE FILM NOIR

Translation:

THOUSAND TIMES BROKEN: THREE BOOKS BY
HENRI MICHAUX

Publications Edited:

VOLT

PEACE

GILLIAN CONOLEY

OMNIDAWN PUBLISHING
RICHMOND, CALIFORNIA
2014

Cover photograph is *Portrait of Space*, by Lee Miller,
taken near Siwa, Egypt, 1937. Gelatin silver print.
14 %16" x 10 ⅚6". © Lee Miller Archives, England, 2013.
All rights reserved.

Book cover & interior design by Cassandra Smith

Offset printed in the United States
by Edwards Brothers Malloy, Ann Arbor, Michigan
on 55# Enviro Natural, 100% recycled, 100% PCW
Acid Free Archival Quality FSC Certified Paper
with Rainbow FSC Certified Colored End Papers

Library of Congress Cataloging-in-Publication Data

Conoley, Gillian, 1955-
[Poems. Selections]
Peace / Gillian Conoley.
    pages cm
ISBN 978-1-890650-95-7 (trade pbk. : alk. paper)
I. Title.
PS3553.O5144P43 2014
811'.54--dc23
                                        2013045789

Published by Omnidawn Publishing, Richmond, California
www.omnidawn.com   (510) 237-5472   (800) 792-4957
            10 9 8 7 6 5 4 3 2 1
            ISBN: 978-1-890650-95-7

For Domenic Stansberry

& Gillis Stansberry

Billie Tom Conoley

& Curby Conoley

& all my friends

& he who rests

Graham Gillis Conoley
(1919–2000)

CONTENTS

an oh   a sky   a fabric   an undertow

an oh   a sky   a fabric   an undertow

a blanket laid upon the grass

all the mixed faces   looking out or looking in   the great paintings

in yard sales and museums   abstract or representational   oils   acrylics   ink

in the poem the evening is spread out

like a media

to let the windbag

out of

        to neutralize

our eternal Footman   who is presidentially nimble

and wears a big gold middle ring   to rap us on the head with

                        when the sky   is a slow moving sea life

a poker tell, the solitary night finches   nested deep, dead asleep

in urban bamboo's

tall corridors

            no longer a president

only an invisible indivisible male muse   all oscuro dark substance

molecularly swarming

in fields in cities   like a cloud rising from sidewalks

                              to make individual appearances

so shaded so shrouded in oil

Whistler could have done him

sometimes appearing   in well-cut overcoat

or next to a tall case clock

to say look this was the deal

made a long time ago

can you give me a ride   to the vacated cities with most hospitable ports

A couple of lonely men had plans that got shoved this way

for a building we could aspire to enter

I donated   then got distracted   for a building we could enter

perhaps we shouldn't   (aspire I mean)

but it is good to build it now, as then

I am entering the poem now   not just to notice the pronoun I

but how casually the no longer   a president has used it

The sky   is a sea

we all committed before sinking into

the most hospitable port   where dust plays dark

before flying   invisibly into

undeadly messengers   done up as citizens

so it's all substance

to make   our children's lives   better than now

a situation I would take

as conduit, as altar

our groceries

there is a lot of room for metaphysics   in this country

I call waiting

the GPS navigational finding device   enhance search   the overly

Google mapped,   severe lack of frontier in the world

so lots of people have begun   exploring the sewers, recording

sounds of manhole covers as cars

roll over them   Only 12 feet down   it feels like 100

and there are rubber boots called   waders but they fill up

quickly   and are discarded   The idea is to tramp

what all gets transformed   back into earth's core

I would like to take some of that infant stardust that has fallen on your head

Why can't I be shrouded in it   if only undercurrent

I used to say my sister sold time on the radio   because that's what she did

but then television leveled

soundscape   the please of the palm tree rustle   in the gelatin print

internet   cresting event   manual or mental   a loose sally of the mind   all of it

suggesting streams   of attenuated speeches by absent friends   who said time

we're no more living   in a landscape   beyond end of the river valley

of that particular program   Now time says   it will save a working copy

of the image   with a slightly different name

My sister and I continue   to run up and down the stairs

Now I will give her a feminine ending

or an infant star fabric   to unfurl   The lonely men

were right to want to fold

their flags back into a triangle   when someone died

We could unfold   and try once more to open

a language in which we do not do

most of the killing

A drop-in date for the ungrievable   Some

will always refuse this country   to come forward

We could all take off our skulls and stare into them   A static in the

contours   rank waterfalls   gray green opal stones   the alert

pianist   key phrases of the Arcadians   Indo-European root-rot   doo-wop

The dead   recircling   rocky crags where recline   the born   or birthing wet

with their last or first words   We could take   our fallen off temperate fur

and begin to recite a Greek story   a groan

now   see how fast   now can go

to what does it matter   world to come   word

to hold in the mouth and swallow

Untapped   what does it mean

if there is no way to say it if you haven't heard it before

so we are all writing writing writing and people say there are too many books

though it seems to be reading that refuses to die   This is the good part

the part looking at the part

Can you tell if this is the good part,

you can tell if this is the good part

if it is the part looking back at you

not wanting to see someone else

airbrushed all over you

It is the feeling of being embodied by the person

you love, or are sweet on, enchanted by—

not that they fill you, but that you

are them, they've come to live inside you,

you look like them

you are so them   you see through them

and imagine they are looking at you,

being them, so

where are you

I am still beautiful

Experiments in Patience I

Vale of soul making—

                      The cotton-top tamarin
                      & the common marmoset
                      approach.

                      The tamarin eats insects
                      with quick jabbing strikes
                      while the common marmoset

                      must wait for days
                      for gum to flow
                      from trees.

Six signs you need to detox—   Patience broods and peacocks

Virtue stirs the pulp

I will wait for the God who hides   the hosannah   of what is received right in my eyes
to escape me

Unfiltered sun
an elevator down

                    a species

                    of dandelions,   yellow splashes

The Patient

I am patient. That is my mineral fact.

    I have long term storage in double helixes

my two long polymers of nucleotides

    my backbone made of sugars and phosphate groups

joined by ester bonds.　I see imagist pears dissolving down

golden arms I hear needle-less the sleep aid cd's

    real violins, then float blue-black

at the eventide, injure

    of the taut to and fro, cut-back

asphalt road, a path of greening twigs nourishing

nothing personal.　Root stocks

    of the best grapes, balm

for the honeybee's bite, lyme's flea—

    money chimes in the community bowl,

with patience I can sit on this bench

and wait for the ironworks of a previous century

    to reverse themselves, or I can lie in the grass,

vision the airplane's scatter-lit

    hallway, the descent

only a little shaky

      like the trouble between art and life rolling you out

onto an unpainted landscape,

the unbelted intoxication of travel   unstable as a chemical's twisted briar

medicine or drug   licit or illicit

or afterimage

time to move along

it's pathos time

dodge a supreme fear

pathos—

        Patience was crowding anxiety

      Patience's gentle tongue was breaking a bone,

      while the twin and drone

      to be patient with

hovered over

our uncharted, rimless wants,

rictus a slit vowel—

                               La vida,
                               a mess of dominoes
                               face down.

I am a pilot light

                               desiring more recognition,

                               I suck grass
                               to the dead inside.

The sleep aid cd & Hippocratic oath   mixed up good

in the cocktail of my head   spoken into like commerce's cavity,

cavity or skylight   opening to the early spring blossoms

in the airless baggage claim

                               SANCHEZ in stencil font
                               stitched to my desert fatigues

holding luggage   looking for someone to pick me up

I can be both
life-charged and dead
in consecutive units,

exited to like

turnpike rest stop's   promisingly lit

pagoda, a respite   for the humans stopping and returning,

the humans predicating,

a human is someone
who has wandered in from the desert.

I am patience in a substance clothed.

truly a creepy troll
truly a creepy troll

a human is the one
continuing to close
Christ's eyes
on the great crucifixes

wagering will there   now be some inevitable progress.   In a tone pour,

the erotics of the electronics   swelling the house
and trailing to the sidewalk,

skip to sound

a harrowing to go, a darned patch

A soft fontanel
a warm harm
a human

does nothing

unusual, forgetting the euphoria
of human potential

is human potential

wanting more tools to form the mind.   Rest, stop, a human is go
stopping and returning,

a practice   a human is someone
to pick you up

a human is someone to hone
in a human's   long-held   desire to vanish   in a crowd or x-ed
out void of others,   in mass human's estranging light.

Experiments in Patience II

Family more
than genetics
and laundry

sweep the earth
in your
cemetery slippers

one foot slipping out

My Mother Moved My Architect

My mother moved
my architect
cutting out newspaper clippings
making the life-long collage
had I sense
I would have
papered the hallways with
instead it is an ephemeral art

a flaxen gene
her left shoulder
out of its socket

will remain that way
rest of days unto nights

what is mentally important

my mother moved my architect
I do not forget
unworn enormous straw hats having gone up in fire
butter churn, too,
a drummer drumming

differently in the hallway all years lead up the stairs
the lingerie

drying on the stairwell
the gait
got the girl in it

The Depression was in the Depression glass

the Carnival plate poised in the window
to seal the light said look

close to see your face

look in the face of your mother
giving way to continuance

redwolfing each nasal fold
and the pearly restitch   in the forehead   what happened there

my mother made
my amazon stockings

made my word order
accordion back   through the binoculars

the woody tendrils of the wisteria
a delicacy on the white pickets
sharpening up   the honeybee riding on that futurity

once my mother's face
spoke it said   let's tear up
our birth certificates and be transubstantiated

make of this world
a planetarium,   ultradense,

what the Big Dipper said to the Little Dipper:

my burial plans include   a new species but first

scatter my ashes
over the grave of your father

be sure to get the right grave
cemetery folks will tell you
this is illegal so do it at night

Midsummer my preference. Box turtle
so still as to look
dead in the middle of the lake.

If one could imagine
a mother between two swans.

Pomegranate   persimmons   shimmering trail of snail
copper nail in the earthen
dank shed
The miscellany began   the perplexity

                                        this drawer
                                        is for kitchen
                                        scissors

peel a grape for a glass eye
bleach kills mildew

toothpaste if no bleach
a kindness brought the pie

I do think at one point
as a woken child I saw
Bonnie and Clyde's car
sleek and perfect   I then understood

God-speed
and if there were any morals I would take Thoreau's

I do not know how the coins got tossed up like that
to fall where they did.

nor the golden piss

      made sheerest.   relieved from a nude.

Look into your mother's face
fount yourself there

forget redemption.
If you want softness, wash your hair in rainwater.

If you crave guidance,
be Virgil to the Dante: *you didn't act this way in the other pit.*

My mother moved my architect
bade fair
she slipped the bolt
upright
like the great sea chest
none of us
had ever seen open

My mother moved my architect
she made it pump and eat

She made this lake
where I come to

over-identify with the dead and call

Dear Echo to my echo,

She made me nude —sheer— and nude again
She made it interesting right up to the end

So that
I have to think what is with

these two heads blurred and blended, this veil
not seen back through

Tail lights,
white gloves with the green stain

as you entered the sunless woods
best to keep the road a little feral where the color is

and your world part dust
fed and unkilled   I am not through
being a poet or a being

What fallen ash
is the power to live

what pituitary
is the grace to keep
doing so

and what good
is temporary measure—

did you say thank you   and were you   thanking

Experiments in Patience III

the speaking machine sits there listening.

a pit and a dungeon.   somebody is not going

to make it in time, but will see you later.

a promissory.

out the window summer voices of children herded

by volunteers.   see you in ten.

how 'bout never?

how does never

sound?

a frayed stylus

brushes the worn-out record's

subcutaneous enormities.

look we've all heard this a million times.

graveyard boots

outside a white shed.

      I love you

beside a small red plastic fork.

sag drags and falls,

Tuscaloosa   greyhound

there are those

who sit in you forever   travelling relics

to escape   the box stores

crows sweep to   typo
                          sky

        [a drawbridge]

see you.   I love you,

but it spills

The small aircraft buffeting the cotton batting you slept on

and couldn't relinquish
its warning was where we wept, and then we stood and then we wept again
through the dark moment of the alder the white containers of the spruce
and the mountains coveting their caves. I had nothing to do with it but
then I tried to come to terms with might I have learned the mountain's
names if you were in the mood for giving them, couldn't you see the way
the earth lay as if waiting for the other planets to slow down to its pace.
Pace, crease, then begin again, heartbeat, pen scratching its way from dare
did I tell you my most innermost secret, did I try to converse at all, no
way to do that trailed my being all the way here, and then I stood apart
and stared. The breath of me kept waning back in and wanting to not
equalize was it longing was it statue, icon or iconography to go so far that
the far became a longitude knowable, a lateral plane where a child could
vanish before coming into the world. Origin is like that, origin is not a
very good friend. Origin is terrifying and peaceful do you imagine that or
troubled. The water is unrippled. A whale has come to lap at the windows
and breach back into the water and disappear even to itself, having as it does
two eyes on either side of its head, gray mass in the middle so it never sees
dead on but instead separately down two different paths that could never
would never connect. So what does it keel toward. Involuntarily our hands
fluttered to touch between pages. What do I know but I can tell you. And
if one can love another then one could do that just fine, without telling it

is something we do, something we come into the world to do. I had not known any bone so hollow or so dug into the earth or piercing up out of the grave like that it was not something I could fully experience like most things we see floating in front of us that we try to hold onto and say wait a minute, won't you stay a minute longer so I can try. I condone clouds. I condone vanilla. A blouse, a stocking. Muddy puddle. The way you could talk about it would be not to talk, not to say one thing that might come to mind. I miss most often if you'd like to come back here. I have a freshly pulled grass hut in which I bury an alternate but not necessarily better childhood's small chipped white porcelain dolls. And there is a bridge, an arc under which one can see the bad river, the pure creek. Two geishas are on a raft, turning their oval faces this way and that, waiting to see what will happen, and when it does, they are no longer waiting they are placidly observing.

PEACE

It fell

      of noon

          weather-like

as in

      a poem the

sudden action of a single word

      you know

         people,

            once you tell them something

                they start talking

[Peace]

smells of sweat deep
in sport-full fields
eyes opened and were thrilled or soothed and sustained
we had won
cars passed along streets in bright difference or decay

[Peace]

in argument context shivers the trigger words
before munitions, oil extracted from the cotton
makes the town smell sweet
no corpus, only body's eidolon
marijuana scented hush of the glove compartment
in your device, a person spies the bridge in flames then flees
so old school, the photo in its bath

[Peace]

contrary to history, to war's punctuations
the almost dripping popsicle held from the body
on the heat-buckled sidewalk, earth's
involuntary memory to descend and ascend,
the round. the blue.
to begin all over again.

4th

of July

bagpipes   big mad Hitchcockian crows

siren   families striding   hurrying

want a whole lot of love   sings the Joplin

mimic   white birch   willow swings   pollen

the cars in shade

way way down gonna give you my love

staying in the house

the crows outside are winning

car door   a muffled crowd gasp   wheels at the top of the sky

and waits

    the night sky's visuals

            called   "Untamed Retribution"   and "Rain Fire"

an objective   sincerity   the war does not space itself

two teenage   girls at the screen   with the sun in their eyes

all day   time takes

all the time   bright canisters in the culverts   girls read

  hills of it

    day-long trash truck heads down our street

what a big

    engine   emergency brake

distance between   telephone pole and queen palm's trunk

        smoke loops   from back of the house to front

    leaves no signet   in cloud   sidewalk's scalding path

                                    'neath county's ripe

                                    corn table

                        globe's eggshell

    for romance   the girls layer their tears back into their skin

            many dawns   the boys waving

        bends

    air crosses clouds in hot nets

            increasing   the local tenor's uprightness

fumes exhume

the crowd stands open-mouthed

heads lifted

you
you
you
you
you
and
you
send me

smoke falls through each head of hair

to each ear's

size and limit

love

sound-chamber'd

moon's

far off

place

[Peace]

　death is to be entered backwards

the necessary condition, a partial vision

at my father's funeral, a blind field

the flag taken from over the casket

folded into a triangle, handed to us

throughout "the reception"

a boy eyes a pizza slice

on a white paper plate

[Peace]

one mystery of the breath: it does not hover
in the body but spirals
and up to two hours   in the less known
mammalian diving reflex   water must be
ice-cold   some people survive
if time began we would do it again
the lungs two oars in the middle of the ocean

[Peace]

interrupting winds
nightfall shifts the lens
we grow still
body sensing itself
why is Maurice Merleau-Ponty
so obsessed with one hand
touching the other one, lips do
as much staying shut
around 6,000 languages

Opened

for Gabrielle Giffords

So it was like sleep and waking, sleep and

fraud on my   Visa, sleep

California

waiting out radioactive plume,

and today another

trying card

in Miami
Winn-Dixie

did they want groceries

or did they want cash, sleep

Freeway sign said   take Lucky Drive

to bypass

bank robbery in shopping mall

so that's where

the two bullets went through.

What sphinx pushes up out the fog in the parking lot

turning each

upon each

our moral imaginations. If it's a gun law,

this tragedy will pull through.

And what was there to   and did she

see, gritty blue sink of desert night sky   with her

off to the side like a wonder, or

your basic hospital room, sleep,

a solitary male nurse, a husband.

Here we pour a new layer, visible

for all to see how we want
          to be as transparent as possible,

     but remain gradient,

dangerous when once it was them,

                    an error, a horror now that it is

What are we to the man

who attacked the gunman

as he started to reload, a constituency?

               Ducks

in the arcade stir a glassy water, sleep, amplify

   Gun with cord tied to it so no one will take it

   The little girl with a hole in her chest

          first girl player to play

in the middle leagues

Gritty blue sunken—shame—as if the desert

could hiss, fold,

The six dead behind her eyelids.   Leave them open,

let us place no more constraints on the eyes of the dead,

illegible cross-outs turned inward,

searching themselves to escape

like figures met in a dream,

she is walking down the hall with a shopping cart

—Never and always

a back to the door—   Whose side—

Once she appears again,

but they won't show her to us

at her husband's launch of four spacewalks

to install the alpha magnetic spectrometer   It will take all four walks

to sift, sleep

through cosmic rays

to define the origin of the universe, though

by now, that plays a minor key.

It could be plutonium, it could be uranium,

we just don't know.

A radioactive plume

to drift over California Friday by noon   a shadow of cloud on the stream

Crows that range and radiate

from cloud to tumbling cloud

And what will she say

privately   and what will she say

in that language of our conviction.

This tragedy will pull through,

and will stand by you tomorrow.

It isn't really heavily radiated water.

How one eye keeps one eye

on a deep and bitter thing.

late democracy

we the undersigned understand then the green of the meadow

has turned to

you who are not my body I vow to you
my resemblance

unequal in value and significance to string my verbal chain:

just let me go out swilling whiskey in the hill country

as imagined and planned.

        who wants to sit around

        worrying about

        third party ads

        on the site

where she and he who is one of them

      (sweet secret green of the yellow)

troll.   they are going to steal my identity:

       metaphysic of a clicking bloom, lotus cup

[Peace]

halftone of a couple in a four poster
who left their breath together
or took too much
white clapboard   distant city
her vagina his cock slack in the cosmological moisture
Christ gets so misquoted
once they put the Latin in him
looking out of the picture wanting nothing

[Peace]

banana tree's garnet/green, transparent
leaf at large in the neighbor's yard
slant, blank in dirt   signs pop up
either an unfathomable mystery   or a no-vote-for-anyone
bus rims the beach   down the aisle
tap tap of the almost silent keyboard
busy fingers of no master
lustre/thunder/empyreal/projecting/nether

[Peace]

if a no more one without the other
could peace and war be a co-presence
peace and war a co-presence
one hand holding another
a metaphysics their separateness a reality
one can no longer touch? we flock to, inflate
death's impatiences

A hatchet with which to chop at the frozen seas inside us

to wake to winter   in the coming out of the time of year

when they release

the masterpieces,

                    but to be still in the other night.

          some drown in movies.

some prefer the unfinished

ungovernable recital,

             a mystical ecology

        where one dies in a camp,

   or rolls out with the dice

          on the sidewalk among boys with

cardboard shields

                and plays dead in white crinoline.

what if paradise was only lifting the veil to flirt.

        no one perfect, but perfection inserts

us so, Pascal

       thinks a God in his pocket.

what if paradise meant walking

          on the ground of our self estrangement,

and the veil of our gaze

       an unsteady balm

was not what we saw through

        but were,   twisting, untwisting—

do you believe.   we were never strictly servants.

Plath and Sexton

there should have been a third
my friends and I

to not feel so incomprehensible
we were carrying your dead books

we were washed in the blood of them
but we were wanting one more

for a while we tried Artaud's "all writing is shit all writers are pigs"

our clubhouse   language   death   war   music   fireflies for an opera

we were thinking a lot about the feminine
we were putting our feminine in a suitcase

and waiting for

caution tape

hyperlinks to take us to
the tulip scape   the blue blazer scape

infinity's integument
undoing

pageboy, if you hold on, we could all be the
third, and you, the task
of our young life,   strangely exhilarated

A Healing for Little Walter

One day we were just lying around trying to key the sound.

Trying to sound the wound, make it bend, loop it through.

Fishbone scar let loose from the forehead,

swim upriver, what touch is to someone alone.

We brought melon and honey, cheap liquor for the task. Gold fill. Gold leaf fill.

Sought sound of a man born in the Crossroads, thirty miles

south, four-corner out near Marksville, Louisiana.

Marksville, Louisiana, with its French signs.

Sound if you wait twelve o'clock a black cat.

Sound if tall man with red eyes appears all you see is red.

Every time you open your mouth, it's red.

What flesh is to bone.

That boy has a nice tone.

Spit easing down

a child's toy come rain. Fish fell from the sky in Marksville, 1947.

Fish fell. We were just lying around trying to key the sound.

Eventually a bone went straight to the forehead.

Small 10-hole Hohner Marine Band harmonica then cheapo harmonica brought to the brink on one easily overloaded, state-owned, then state-discarded,

public address amplifier.

Sound that removed our heads from our backsides, sound

we could lay in, drape, then pour its honey onto

and glisten with, the spiderweb left at the dark Apollo.

Marksville population 5,537

at 2000 census, total area 4.1 square miles, of which

10.6 km² is land, 0.24%, water.

Where once was the Crossroads.

Marksville, Louisiana with its French signs.

Let us break down the farm of Louis Leviage on Drupines Road.

Knock on the door of the shotgun shack beside.

Death our greatest front man.

That and a bullet-shaped microphone.

The humble mouth organ.

Once harmonica 25 cents after Little Walter 10 dollar.

Today even jackhammer got the juke

cracking up pipeline breaking through wall into sun again.

Instrument saying to its player, thanks man, thanks Marion Walter Jacobs.

What flesh is to bone you must pass to pass through.

Sprinkle sachet powders down deep personal valleys.

Breaking through wall into sun again

Tina knew how to Turn and Run.

Carla got the ropy veins.

Knocking on the door of the shotgun shack beside.

What flesh is to bone.

Every time you open your mouth, it's red.

What he did, he took advantage of himself being himself, on himself, you know?

Sashay Little Walter.

What flesh is to bone.

High rolling, passing through.

Gold fill. Gold leaf fill. Thereby shall we have increase of the light.

Liquor golden. Knife shut. How men get. Fist pulled back and stuck into pocket.

Head from your backside. Forehead smoothed. Gold fill. Gold leaf fill.

That isn't Death in the middle that's a minor stream.

A tall man with red eyes appears all you see is red.

That isn't breath on the downside that's another minor stream.

That boy has a nice tone.

A public address amplifier thereby shall we have increase of the light.

Small 10-hole Hohner Marine band harmonica

cheapo harmonica then Little Walter

holding a black cat before a man with a white cane.

Fish fell. Four corners spread wide open. Stab wounds in the dirt.

Knocking on the door of the shotgun shack beside. Gold fill. Gold leaf fill.

Carla and Tina rose and fell

Tina still rising.

A blue peal bent so far back it's red.

Little Walter, beasts looking solemn at you

from the other side.

Tina still rising.

Turn and Run.

Gold fill,

Gold leaf fill.

Fishbone thereby shall we see the light.

A silver pickup at the yellow end.

Like gold into scar

a twister in the skull.

    Fish scales

      rising in the tub

      and the river.

      A beast's molecular

      snore and drone

      on the other shore.

      Carla rising

      running with Tina.

      A masterhood

      that bet

      you missed a note

      and grooved thereby.

      Now a carven turkey

      once a wild hoot

a harmonica clung to

and fell from.

Carla rising running with Tina.

What he did.

Like gold into scar a twister in the skull.

Thank you, man.

Beast looking solemn at the sun shown up for supper.

Knives lifting the four corners

shook out chains molt to moebius a pierce into the blueness.

Turn, and Run.

Cetripedal, centripetal.

Gold fill, gold leaf fill.

Crying and wailing with our toy harmonicas

in a space gone unbolt into

a blueness sucking in the sun

sun on the liquor golden

sun down the farm

sun on the door of the shotgun

your mouth it's red

to bone.

to bone.

sun on the spit easing down.

       pipeline through wall.

       every time you open

       instrument saying

       thereby shall we

       someone alone

     One day

     sun down deep

     what flesh

     fell from

break down

the

forehead

   the

   sky

every time

touch is

day

you open your mouth

pass through

Sun's Rift

Some of the soldiers are real, and some of the soldiers are fictive.
We can see, or brush in, a cloud, puffy and likeable.
We could see which soldier might
ask us to dance,

     which figure each would prefer,

our actual or our shadow.

Into, on   ever goes   the buzz saw, hammer,
trunk slam. Board   sheer wall   deck   eventually become
a kind of company.

Still pall through the square for the window,

     hot shroud across our backs.

Sun ungraved,   braved, star without night, convective

     plasma,

        wonder in a nest

at the window's black net

               (best shadow

               a dog's bark,   earthly)

In the informal, a yellow dwarf.   Light falls   sun
to earth   in about
8 minutes, 19 seconds.

     Currently travelling   the local

interstellar cloud,

the sun is in the bubble zone   within the inner rim

of the Orion arm

of the Milky Way, which it orbits

clockwise, bracelet-like, once

every 250 million years, that's how

slow it is. The sun has only 5.4 billion years left,

all highly eventful   and unimaginable.

Satin

doll spits and swarms   into its own face,   arcing   flame-loop,

corona   hollow   crown,   then head   again, ball, reliquary

bloodletting skyward,   greening down, across,   then comes

the Red Giant phase.

When due to its tidal interactions,

Earth will be incinerated,

or ripped

of what thread that keeps things so.

Our actual or our shadow.

Soldiers dance a carcass.

A face disappears, once it comes closer. Burnished coil or golden hair.

To aim is to come home.

To sleep under a tree, or to swing there.

Whole cluster of faces, none seen all at once.

I am writing an article (Johnny Cash)

I am writing an article for the Sunday magazine.   I am 23, I have my face

made up, feeling smoke where the tongue slides,

                              smoke while carrying around a camera

like I know what to do living through Dallas without actually being in

Dallas   feeling warm and sunned on

when he walks out of bad B movie trailer   with black eternal hair

            careers.   want a career,   I do,   careers come to

worse. some try to   run out of amphetamines   in the seven seas,

in the backyard hut   we call our own.   no more

shall I wear that old black dress,   greasy all around.   no more shall I

wear the old black bonnet   with holes all in the crown.

            Christ newly staked and writhing

in the heart   in the door-wide chest   in the overall

black tower of you   (I would have been scared

of you,   if I didn't have the camera   —now dangling by my side—

if *didn't*   didn't cast such a great divide)

                didn't mean   who what where when how

in a free song

did you become a long pendulous cipher   listing leanwards out the door

with one hand turned to dusk,   the other down, free

          pine

     trees.

     pretty nightgown   to sleep beside.   daybreak's

got film   to track, a when   where to walk out

of,   to bring one's instrument   and not repeat,   how

draw back your kimono,   when take out

your .44,   boots

for quadribeat.

the camera cries.   (two noon-bound yellow jackets floating backwards

                              into calmer vectors   off the trailer's side.)

                    I drop   the crisp green-lined

reporter notebook,   blank clean empty as Mallarmé,   how walk away, my

Walkaway. with one   long-stemmed carnation

careers do godless things.   leave your father's

house, dewfall upon the world.

                      what makes a shaken figure

on bust-up white concrete   shiver again,

who carved

face of faceless thing

how   what

did a blue black sky

                          leech in, crow down,   increase.

Monday Morning

everything was on sale   the pop music was under the heat lamps

and the spectacle was on the television

and the television was in the spectacle

the life that is at least ¾ automatism   said to the life

that isn't   just look

at the great big burden of you   quit mail   quit mail

Beyoncé   (Beyoncé put a ring on it check it out youtube)

try to live as though it were morning,   said Nietzsche

can we show off the backbends in the yoga class   and still progress

that is a very optimistic statement of Nietzsche's

it was morning and all the white guilt got balled up

and tossed through the sky then landed back

into the white guilt which had made   a very good deal with the white privilege

and the light through the burnt-out leaf pattern   in the curtain fabric

fell to the hands spread-eagle   on the yoga mat   pushing hard

one friend called and said "here we are"   and I said   "here we are"

and the hand picked up the garden hose curled in the calla lilies drips of water in the copper snout   and giovanni called and said it never

occurred to me there WOULDN'T be a black president why is everyone calling me

to congratulate   ME I didn't do a thing   I know a lot of black people

with good jobs   look there's one   says giovanni   with a bad cold

who was born after the Civil Rights Movement   so I point that   out to her

and she says yeah right   my last cousin not in prison just went to prison

nothing's over   so I look at my hand no longer spread on the yoga mat

same hand that slapped hands wiped up shit stacked money cut the vegetables

and filled in the dot   *Cinderella, Camelot*   the white guilt said to the white guilt

don't you even try to feel better now   you still have to

wake up in the morning and live as though it were morning

you can give yourself a little release more breath a very large exhale through the mouth

you done good girl   you can go to the grocery store   you can look

into the black faces   you encounter   everywhere in all the jobs

good and bad and they look back at you   a little different now

you can't say what it is   you can't describe it

but you can observe it   if you can stay aware long enough   every morning

it is the morning you can try to live   as though it were morning

the ghost wars   whispering to the ghost wars   their Miranda rights

the white privilege starting the car   trying out the back seat

knuckle bone   flat palm   pinkie   finger wide

here we are   here we are

try to live as though it were morning

light on the hands   spread eagle   breathe and the white guilt said   hold   hold

Trying to Write a Poem about Gandhi

I.

The future leaves roses on the bed

for the long stretch of the waker

at the window left to pull

the day around.   History props up and swarms a lot of time.

Wonder will he walk back.   Should we still run to keep up with him.

Fingers quick to thread the spinning wheel.

A dizziness in the face

of a social machine.

      Silver, infinitesimal motes   shine lift and hover-cloud

I shake out the dryer's lint drawer

        into garage air—*satyagraha,*

no power over the soul

the body suffers

II.

A silver pocket watch pinned to a loincloth

      Better to hand wash

In past and in future   Postmodernism's gone all artisan

                    motes swirling up into stale garage air

Open door   to let it   drift out   spread into wisteria's tresses

          ahimsa,

a matter not of the intellect

but of the heart

III.

Beloved figures die

                    then stop and loop

to pixelate,

a history sweeps and fells the picture field.   In uppermost

loamy branches of the giant oak

sit Thoreau, Tolstoy, Ruskin, Emerson and Carlyle.

Shining down their texts.

Unorthodox social moralists of the 19th century

still trying to freeze hell.

Many leafy wandering past participles in my neighborhood alone.

Also one assault rifle, a shotgun, two Glock pistols

one tactical armored vest   How do I know this   several gas masks

one child's ballistic leggings   ballistic helmet

one known pedophile

Best to try not to wish anyone

dead, think John Berryman, "I woke up, and I had not murdered anyone,"

before I turn back to the dryer, thinking why think   or try to be like Marx

who said at the end of his life, I am not a Marxist.

That's my girl's lost blue sweater hung on the fencepost.

Best to think of even nuisances

in your inbox

                              as pilgrims on earth, immortal spirits on probation.

IV.

How to make of one's garden a Tolstoy Farm.

And be chief magistrate, prime minister,

main teacher, chief baker, chief sanitary inspector

of a modest magnetic field produced by electric currents in earth's outer core, on earth's

crust primarily quartz (silicon dioxide) and other silicates like feldspar.

One too bright day, here comes Manu and Abha.

Manu—grandniece, and Abha—wife of grandnephew—

Gandhi's "girls" and "walking sticks," his hands

on their shoulders as he walked everywhere with them toward the end.

Poverty easy   but chastity eludes
and means

        funny sleeping arrangements—

            younger and younger naked girls to sleep

                beside

        to "maintain" chastity

               brahmcharya,

    elimination of all desire
        in the face of temptation

Accept the body!
You pussy,   picture field says dropping down

      great thinkers or/
      scheming demotic despots it's a thin line
      to undo and silly
      to be an apologist for a pacifist

        Dale Carnegie   ✓friend

    Madame Blavatsky   ✓friend

Why think
God doesn't like
          pussies, cocks, girls, Gandhis   all together

well, you'd have to ask the girls,
and later

          It's a sub-rosa geological planet, with shifting hot mantels of tectonics,
someone should tell Einstein—
even though it's too late—who said,
"Future generations will hardly grasp that
such a man as this walked upon the earth."

Palm fronds for shade.

                    Basil, peppers, early tomatoes here.

Strawberries under chicken wire to frustrate deer.

 In the garden, motes and mites,
                    all waxes and wanes
in shadows' leafy deep sea ocularity.

The future drags and drifts and lifts   traces of argon, carbon dioxide and water,
sun's majestic past and impending

life. "You cannot hope to wake anyone who isn't fully asleep"

          he said

"you cannot wake those who are *pretending* sleep"

Where the page was, do we walk

                    into the blown

            door frame

        atonal   soaked in cloud   our obsolete

          hands reaching but not reached   and pushing glass away

more room now

                        clear nectar

for the happy Graces

                        walking in

                            the white glow

        curling along

                calla lilies

                which flute and sway

with their austere

        good looks

                              If we take

our power to the next
power

                                                  to the silence
                                                  on the other end

                                                  do we say hello

clear nectar to the happy Graces their disassociating hands more hands to reach for in the
flowering fibrous grasses

where the page was

                    a white she-goat

                    we laugh over

                              Do we pick up   glass

                                        do we

          take   silence

               a car fast   through a flood

throwing sheets of water

                              to the next car

                              blinding temporarily

                              struck in the white glow

If we look from our page up

          to sun

                              how to permit voyage

                              going for source

                              and from it

Time

                    confabulates

               the whistler: a mother in the grocery store   her coral lips

                              an embarrassment doing

                                   birds   a partial Sinatra

would we rather   she chew gum   or throw pearls

in the dishwashing

liquid. do we fill

each empty dress.

if black coal hair was our mother's like the bare-breasted island beauties of Guam

a father brought home

photos of

after war do we stare

at them, a child stung under dinner's

table. later our bare smooth

teenage legs rushing past

put boyhood friend on acid back

into car drive him

to airport to some

base   then Nam

his draft number   was One

sun

sun

Do we leave

   nectar

to the flowering

do we have

    Grace

if we try to be more holy

take care the screen in the church parlor

sip the nectar's

            tissue-like   contour

            the guiltless guilt of whole cloth thick, lit as if

            wax paper drapes the

pear tree

steady, short

still flowering not about to fruit

      If we look from a page

          sun curling over what

do we want

to point out   or paint   time is lost

                                        unwaving

            light

                        storm's

blizzard

            a car fast through flood

        throws sheets of water

                        to the next car

                        blinding temporarily

the happy Graces cutting shade providing chambers with their disassociating hands

more hands to reach for in the flowering fibrous grasses in the white widening white

Tenderness of the Dove

tender or tinder   put me in one   a box

with velvet lining

stay the glove

to warm the hand

quivering masterfully the fishes etched in lime

downriver, thick with stream

it was too quiet to hear the ringing

and yet we wed   a changeling   to a trifling

a red sweater   was my love   a color rinsed my hair

a guitar

we all gave out   playing

Toughness of the Serpent

I think maybe we should take out 10 or 12 of them

      just to show that we are serious, says E. D. Nixon to MLK.

Montgomery's steam fallen into leafiness, warm midnight temper

                of faucet water. Transfigurative green Cadillac

of one Mrs. A. W. West

              catching the dew in her carport.

Dreaming-in-waking   blood brotherhood of those tried to live paradise

           buses empty

              in the recessive spaces.

MLK really tired at this point.

Wonder what he's got on his mental sky.

        Moon yellow scorch of the morning iron, serene, serene

occupied

remaster, I got big sign I amble off

face lit as skin of someone bathing.

young frayed hoods smell saltier.

police refuse the stairs, one gropes a breast

under a sports bra. historical pic! crowd

shoots all then closes behind, laptop.

you sexy thang. anticrow anticrow

anticrows and swoops

the street, imperfectible, police seem

to have insatiable sexual

appetites, skyscraper bends over itself, as if to bow

or readjust, then lighthouses

a tangerine rolling out of a tent

is a real tangerine and people are

intemperate, out of air current   hot breath and other waves

of Being, wherein each calls for the other,

gives a sign. how to lift

the limit between the body and the world—

birds cry!   lovers die!

hermit can't eat the plastic

the sports bra snaps back

of great design

vet of bones all his brothers dead inside him stops to pose

with the lean of a milkman, smiles his truths of 1945.

the policeman's hand is gone

imaginal, archetypal

the best messages are mutual and free from all ambition, like a wishbone.

hermit licks the wrapper.

Steve Jobs we're sorry you died

images feel good taken into the human palm.

how to back into our new instruments

how light November rain

Begins

begins with sound of bell
ends with briefcase dark
glorying day's pantomime
I feed on color
I take the symbols turn them over
I don't understand a thing
when I look, I sturdy the thread
on the lake, form
when I look, a face
a living unity recomposed

my beloveds cannot unwire

in time for dinner

against these couches these islands they roam

the hallway's blur

nothing holds at this exposure

I didn't want my eyes to be

my reality negator

thick black plastic laid down over weeds
bewitched female mass
Spinoza tells us the animals walk solitary
in the rain and do not question
being whole   I cannot
see and it is irritating me
memory rains all over my family
memory rains all over my work

slow cool of the ice in my cheek

I am ashamed that I would like to see inside

the skull of my daughter

and fix everything

I am ordinary and alone

a bosomy female figure appears

behind the screen door

the smell of parrots

a ribbon falls

from my daughter's hair

onto her plastic town

in the big green and athletic fields
one could imagine a particularly
rigorous amount of fucking
at my gate, the saturated
mildly hysterical birds of paradise
stare one into the other

I am committed to the visual
though I like talking, too
and wearing several pairs
of glasses, that is like
the description of a film
one pupil never sees the other though
both may shift and roam
likewise the dirt was fine, moist and coal black
good to grow up, around, and in

the history came along unyielding and in ill-repair

a system I walked but could not climb

I met uncertain people with untaught

though fully absorbed vernaculars

a waft of baking on the sidewalks

on the porches the cloudless simplicities

to stay the field I strode my modern town hard into the falling rain

I was running really hard away as if to stumble forward

I was one big block shape

I was many folded into a sweater

I had a great desire to see myself now as a mother to that image

and build further a humility of splendidness

a riot of spirit I could die into and leap toward and for in joy

if the middle range would have me now
would permit me
a particularly Blakean protein
lodged too deep in my psyche and that's
what is wrong with me
if when I look out I am turning on that subjectivity
geodesic and unlikely
hungry the narcissistic ego would find a way
to get out of the pathological books
I love dancing because it makes me feel
strong and beautiful
and made of muscle and air
it is a weedy, unmanicured trail

Kandinsky said an object was a narrative

and so he disapproved of it

de Kooning said you are with a group or movement

because you cannot help it

I just wanted a church we could go to

or stand in front of and beg

to allow something to remain potential

so the eyes wouldn't hate their little dictators

for one eye, a small Mesopotamian figure

for one eye, a big abstract

I look, and your face is like a part of speech not spoken

a tragedy so near its comic ash

one eye is my future, one eye, my mausoleum

the divine in what is seen

in which we view only the shade of

possibility: a semi-reluctant scribe I read her book trembling

scattered in every territory
as one of the visibles this dispatch
sun I wish you
each euphoriant ephemery
everything ought
to keep on going
I imagine my life

Acknowledgments

Much gratitude to the editors of magazines where many of these poems first appeared: *The Brooklyn Rail*, *Colorado Review*, *Conjunctions*, *Drunken Boat*, *Eleven Eleven*, *Fence*, *jubilat*, *The Kenyon Review*, *The Massachusetts Review*, *New American Writing*, *New Orleans Review*, *Occupy Writers*, *99 Poems for the 99 Percent*, *Poem-A-Day*, *Textsound*, *The Academy of American Poets*, *The Offending Adam*, and *Your Impossible Voice*. Special thanks to Brian Teare of Albion Books, Andrew Wessels of *The Offending Adam*, and Naropa Institute of Disembodied Poetics for making beautiful chapbooks and broadsides of some of these poems. Appreciation and wonder to Brian Lucas for including poems in *Poetbook (BOOK #2)*. In great gratitude and thanks to Rusty Morrison, Ken Keegan, and everyone at Omnidawn for their care and fortitude.

Notes

"Opened" contains several phrases repeated on news radio following Japan's March 11, 2011 earthquake, tsunami, and meltdown of three nuclear reactors. The poem also contains phrases from President Barack Obama's speech after six people were killed in an open meeting in a Safeway parking lot where Representative Gabrielle Giffords also suffered a gunshot wound to the head, January 8, 2011. "A Healing for Little Walter" is for painter and printmaker Hawley Hussey and was inspired by her linoleum print *Blue Lonesome: A Healing for Little Walter*, and, consequently, by *Blues with a Feeling: The Little Walter Story*. In "I am writing an article (Johnny Cash)," the line "No more shall I wear the old black dress..." is from the old folk song "The Factory Girl." In "Plath and Sexton," "blue blazer" refers to Sexton's blue jacket bequeathed to poet Maxine Kumin, who mentions it in her poem "How It Is": "the dumb blue blazer of your death." In "Begins," ideas of Wassily Kandinsky and Willem de Kooning are from de Kooning's *Collected Writings*. "A hatchet with which to chop at the frozen seas inside us" is Kafka.

photo by Gillis Stansberry

Gillian Conoley was born in Austin, Texas, where, on its rural outskirts, her father and mother owned and operated a radio station. She is the author of seven collections of poetry, including PEACE, THE PLOT GENIE, PROFANE HALO, LOVERS IN THE USED WORLD, and TALL STRANGER, a finalist for the National Book Critics Circle Award. Her work has received the Jerome J. Shestack Poetry Prize from *The American Poetry Review*, a National Endowment for the Arts grant, and a Fund for Poetry Award. Her poems have been anthologized widely, most recently in W.W. Norton's *Postmodern American Poetry*, *Norton's American Hybrid*, and *Best American Poetry*. A poet, editor, and translator, Conoley has taught as a visiting writer at University of Denver, the Iowa Writers' Workshop, Tulane University, and Vermont College. Her translations of Henri Michaux, THOUSAND TIMES BROKEN: THREE BOOKS BY HENRI MICHAUX, will appear with City Lights in 2014. Editor and founder of *Volt*, she is Professor and Poet-in-Residence at Sonoma State University. She lives with her family in a small town just north of San Francisco.

Peace
by Gillian Conoley

Cover text set in Avenir LT Std.
Interior text set in Garamond 3 LT Std and Avenir LT Std.

Cover photograph is *Portrait of Space*, by Lee Miller,
taken near Siwa, Egypt, 1937. Gelatin silver print.
14 9/16" x 10 5/16". © Lee Miller Archives, England, 2013.
All rights reserved.

Cover & interior design by Cassandra Smith

Offset printed in the United States
by Edwards Brothers Malloy, Ann Arbor, Michigan
on 55# Enviro Natural, 100% recycled, 100% PCW
Acid Free Archival Quality FSC Certified Paper
with Rainbow FSC Certified Colored End Papers

Omnidawn Publishing
Richmond, California
2014

Rusty Morrison & Ken Keegan, Senior Editors & Publishers
Cassandra Smith, Poetry Editor & Book Designer
Gillian Hamel, Poetry Editor & *OmniVerse* Managing Editor
Sara Mumolo, Poetry Editor
Peter Burghardt, Poetry Editor & Book Designer
Turner Canty, Poetry Editor
Liza Flum, Poetry Editor & Social Media
Sharon Osmond, Poetry Editor & Bookstore Outreach
Juliana Paslay, Fiction Editor & Bookstore Outreach Manager
Gail Aronson, Fiction Editor
RJ Ingram, Social Media
Pepper Luboff, Feature Writer
Craig Santos Perez, Media Consultant